Inventions

Great Ideas and Where They Came From

by Sarah Houghton

Reading Consultant:
Timothy Rasinski, Ph.D.
Professor of Reading Education
Kent State University

Content Consultant:
Erik Swanson
The Inventors Museum

Red Brick™ Learning

Published by Red Brick™ Learning
7825 Telegraph Road, Bloomington, Minnesota 55438
http://www.redbricklearning.com

Library of Congress Cataloging-in-Publication Data
Houghton, Sarah, 1978–
    Inventions: great ideas and where they came from/by Sarah Houghton.
    p. cm.—(High five reading)
    Includes bibliographical references (p. 46) and index.
    Summary: Highlights inventions and inventors throughout history and
discusses why people invent and the steps in the inventive process.
    ISBN 0-7368-9532-9 (Paperback)—ISBN 0-7368-9554-X (Hardcover)
    1. Inventions—Juvenile literature. [1. Inventions.] I. Title. II. Series.
T48 .H738 2002
609—dc21

                        2002000192

Created by Kent Publishing Services, Inc.
Executive Editor: Robbie Butler
Designed by Signature Design Group, Inc.

Printed in the United States of America.

3 4 5 6 08 07 06 05 04 03

Table of Contents

Lewis Latimer

Archimedes

Faces of
Invention

Marie Curie

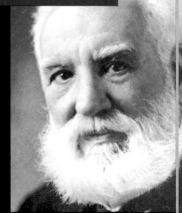

Alexander Graham Bell

CHAPTER 1

How Inventors Invent

Have you ever had a great idea for an invention? Have you ever seen something and thought, "Hey, that was my idea"? Well, maybe some day you will be a great inventor!

Inventions Are Everywhere

Have you heard of Thomas Edison? He invented the light bulb. How about Lewis Latimer? He and Joseph Nichols invented the filament that burns inside the light bulb. Without them, Edison's light bulb would not have worked well.

We live in a world filled with inventions. But who thought of all these bright ideas? People from all over the world invent. Some are young, and some are old. Some create new things; others make old things better. Some are famous. Some never will be.

---

filament: the fine thread that glows inside a light bulb

Thomas Alva Edison

Thomas Alva Edison was born in the United States in 1847. He was kicked out of school because his teachers said he was a slow learner. In fact, Edison had hearing problems.

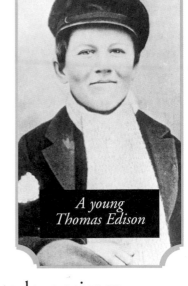

A young Thomas Edison

Edison's mother decided to teach him at home. She taught him to love science. When he was 10, Edison built his own laboratory. Then he began to invent. He patented an amazing 1,093 inventions. Some include:

- the electric light bulb
- a machine to record sound
- a movie camera
- a typewriter

---

laboratory: a special room where scientific work is done
patent: to get a legal record that says an invention is your own idea, and that you invented it first

How Inventors Work

How do inventors come up with ideas? First, they usually try to find out what people already know. They research to learn what has worked in the past. They also study what has failed. This way they make fewer mistakes.

Edison had many interests. One was helicopters. Leonardo da Vinci (LEE-oh-nar-doh duh-VEN-chee) drew plans for the first helicopter in 1400. But da Vinci never built his. More than 500 years later, Heinrich Focke, a German, invented the first helicopter to really fly. That was in 1936.

But long before Focke's success, Edison researched the helicopter. He looked at the helicopter designs of inventors such as da Vinci. Edison also researched engines and ways to power them. He put together all the facts he learned.

---

research: to study and find out about something

Think, Plan, and Do

After inventors research, they think. They think about what they have learned. Inventors want to be able to predict how an experiment might work out. This prediction is called an *hypothesis*.

For example, Edison researched ways to power engines. He knew that gunpowder explodes. The force of the explosion powers bullets from guns. He wondered if the same force could power a helicopter engine. Edison decided to explore this idea.

Most inventors record their plans. They write down any methods they will use. This helps them to think clearly about each step. A plan helps inventors to spot any dangers or other problems their work may cause. A plan also makes a record. This record can help others later on.

---

predict: to say what you think might happen
experiment: a scientific test to try out an idea or to see the effect of something
method: a way of doing something

Edison planned how he would make and test his new engine. He would have to be careful. Otherwise, there might be surprise fireworks! Once he had a careful plan, he could do the experiments.

Thomas Edison in his laboratory

Observe and Record

Inventors make careful notes on what they observe. They write down everything that happens. Even the smallest event they record. Those notes might be helpful later.

Edison observed something he did not expect. The gunpowder blew up. So did the engine. So did the laboratory! His reaction was simple. He gave up the idea that he might power an engine with gunpowder.

After an experiment, inventors have another task. They record how and why they reacted. Such a record helps inventors remember what they did. It also helps other inventors find out what happened and why. People can use that record to form a better plan for other experiments.

No one has tried to make a gunpowder-powered engine again. Why might that be?

---

observe: to watch something
reaction: an action in response to something

The Process of Inventing

REACT

RECORD

OBSERVE

DO

PLAN

THINK

RESEARCH

CHAPTER 2

Inventions Through History

Imagine a world with no wheels.
What would it be like? Think of all
the things you know that use some
kind of wheel. How many can you list?

TIME LINE: Prehistory to A.D. 900

2.5 million years ago first tools	10,500 B.C. pottery vessels	6000 B.C. bricks	4000-3500 B.C sailing boats

3000 B.C.: The Wheel

At one time, there were no wheels. Someone had to invent the wheel.

You might think a wheel is the simplest invention. But it is also one of the most important. Some people believe the wheel was invented around 5,000 years ago.

The first wheels came from Mesopotamia (MESS-uh-puh-TAME-ee-ah). This area is now in modern Iraq. Some early wheels were made from stone. Others were just slices from tree trunks.

Today we have thousands of types of wheels. How were all these wheels invented? Inventors observed how the first wheels worked. They thought of other uses for wheels. They tried their ideas out. If an idea worked, a new wheel was invented.

3500 B.C. plow	600 B.C. coins	A.D. 105 paper	A.D. 600-900 gunpowder

A.D. 1340: The Renaissance

Starting in about 1340, a time of great invention began. It lasted for more than 300 years. During this period, people began to think, write, draw, and explore more than ever before.

People call this period "the Renaissance." *Renaissance* means "rebirth." It was as if the world was born again with new ideas, art, and inventions.

One very important Renaissance invention was the printing press. The printing press had a huge effect on people. Books became less expensive. Now, common people could learn to read and write by studying these books.

TIME LINE: **A.D. 900 to 1600**

| **About 1450** printing press | 1500 watch | 1520 violin |

Between 1438 and 1454, the printing press with moveable type was invented by Johannes Gutenberg.

1565
pencil

1590
microscope

1596
flushing toilet

15

1760: Skating into History

Ice skates were invented at least 2,000 years ago. But the first roller skates were made only about 250 years ago. The first roller skate maker worked in London in the 1760s. His name was Joseph Merlin.

Merlin wanted to show everyone how great his skates were. He decided to skate into a grand ball. He planned to play the violin as he skated.

---

ball: a large, formal dancing party

TIME LINE: **A.D. 1600 to 1850**

1620	1705	1709
submarine	steam engine	piano

Merlin entered the room as planned. Suddenly, he realized his invention was not quite complete. He had forgotten to add brakes!

Merlin rolled across the room playing. But when it came time to stop, he couldn't. He wanted to grab on to something. But he had the violin in his hands. Finally, he did stop—when he crashed into a huge mirror.

Other inventors improved Merlin's skates. They added brakes. The brakes made it easier to go around corners. In 1863, an American inventor added shock absorbers. This made the ride smoother. Roller skates became very popular.

---

shock absorber: something that lessens the effect of a jarring force

1800	1839	1840
battery	bicycle	postage stamps

1956: Velcro™

In 1956, a man named Georges de Mestral was walking his dog. He noticed small plants, called *beggar's-lice*, sticking to the dog's coat. Later, he looked at the beggar's-lice under a microscope. He could see tiny hooks. These hooks made the beggar's-lice stick to the dog's fur.

De Mestral wanted to make his own version of beggar's-lice. He studied how the hooks worked. He figured out how they made the beggar's-lice stick. He thought about how to make his own hooks.

---

beggar's-lice: a plant with dry, prickly seed pods that stick to fur and clothing
version: a form of something

TIME LINE:	**1850 to NOW**		
1876 telephone	**1885** car	**1894** radio	**1903** Teddy bear

18

De Mestral did many experiments. Each time he recorded the results. He reacted to those results by trying to improve his fake beggar's-lice. He studied and worked on the invention for eight years. Finally, he had it. De Mestral had invented Velcro™.

We don't know what will be invented next. We don't know who will invent it. It might be anyone. It might be you!

The seed pods of beggar's-lice

1928	1946	1969	1982	2010
antibiotics	microwave oven	jumbo jet	compact disc	Who knows?

CHAPTER 3

Why Inventors Invent

Have you ever wished for a machine that made your bed? If you were an inventor, you might try to invent one. Inventors create things for many reasons. Do you have any idea what those reasons might be?

FIG. 1095.—Straight Microscopic Forceps.

FIG. 1096.—Curved Microscopic Forceps.

FIG. 1097.—Hard Rubber Microscopic Syringe.

FIG. 1094.—Spear-Pointed Microscopic Knife.

FIG. 1098.—Brass Microscopic Syringe.

To obtain fluid contained in pleural, pericardial or abdominal cavity, &c., for examination, the Aspirators are useful.

Inventing to Meet Needs

Often, inventors create things to meet needs. This means they think of something they or someone else needs. Then they figure out how to make it. They follow the "research, think, plan, do, observe, record, react" steps. The hypodermic syringe was invented in this way.

Until 1853, doctors and nurses gave drugs as pills. But some drugs work better if they go straight into the blood. Inventors wanted to find a way to make this happen.

C. Pravaz met this need in 1853. He invented the hypodermic syringe. This hollow needle could send medicine straight into the bloodstream.

---

hypodermic syringe: a hollow needle used to give injections under the skin

Inventing by Accident

Some inventions are not planned. An inventor might be looking for one thing and find something else by accident. But the surprise invention may be really useful anyway.

During World War II (1939–45), America needed more rubber. For a long time, inventors had been trying to make rubbery material from silicone. Silicone comes from sand. There was plenty of sand. But silicone was gooey. Inventors wanted to make it harder.

James Wright was working on this problem. He had silicone in a test tube when he accidentally dropped some acid on it. He wondered what the acid would do to the silicone.

---

silicone: a substance found in sand and rocks
test tube: a narrow glass tube closed at one end and used to hold liquids
accidentally: by mistake

Wright took some of the mixture out of the test tube. When he dropped it, it bounced right back! He pulled it. He stretched it. The stuff kept going back to its former shape. But bouncing putty wasn't going to help America win the war.

Bouncing putty was fun, though. Soon everyone was talking about it. One man started selling it in plastic eggs. It became very popular. By 1968, Silly Putty™ had even gone into space. Apollo 8 astronauts took it with them to the moon.

Another scientist, Earl Warrick, also claimed that he invented Silly Putty™. Like Wright, Warrick said he invented it by accident. Whoever invented it, Silly Putty™ was an accident worth millions of dollars!

---

mixture: something made up of different things mixed together

A Moldy Cure

Some inventions happen by accident *and* meet a need. Alexander Fleming, a Scottish scientist, had such a useful accident.

Fleming knew that infections killed many people each year. He knew that germs cause infections. One day in 1928, he had been doing some experiments in which he grew germs on dishes. Fleming planned to add different chemicals to the germs. He would watch what each chemical did to the germs. He wanted to learn which chemicals could kill the germs.

Later, Fleming looked at the dishes where he had grown the germs. He noticed mold growing on the dishes. He hadn't washed them in time!

Then he noticed something else—the mold was killing the germs. He couldn't believe it. His discovery was made completely by accident.

---

infection: an illness caused by a germ or virus
chemical: a substance produced in chemistry

Fleming started to grow mold on purpose. Other scientists helped. Together, they made antibiotics. These are drugs that are made from a special mold. Antibiotics fight some infections.

Antibiotics have saved millions of people's lives. You have probably taken them yourself.

Moral: Don't wash the dishes!

Alexander Fleming in his laboratory

antibiotic: a drug that cures some infections and diseases

The Weird and the Wacky

Some inventions happen because of a need. Some happen by accident. Some happen for both reasons. And some inventions are so weird, you wonder why they happened at all!

On the worldwide web you can find a site all about weird inventions. For example, you can read about "Deer Ears." The inventor of Deer Ears says they will help you hear better. You can also find "The Criminal Truth Extractor." Someone patented this crime-fighting invention in 1930. The Criminal Truth Extractor creates a spooky image of a ghost. It is supposed to scare criminals into confessing!

Also on this web site, you can find "Toilet Landing Lights." These lights help you see the toilet in the dark. Happy landings!

---

criminal: someone who does something against the law
extractor: a machine that takes something out of something else
confess: to admit that you did something wrong

Do these inventions meet a need?

The flying bike of 1905

This fan mount was invented in 1945.

Did they happen by accident?

A robot that washes your car was invented in 1975.

Were they good ideas?

Check out other wacky inventions at http:/www.totallyabsurd.com.

This painting is based on a
Greek myth about a father and son
who make wings to fly. Here, the father
watches the son as he falls from the sky.

CHAPTER 4

They Wanted to Fly

Humans have always wanted to fly. The oldest stories in the world tell of people who tried to fly. Most of them failed. Some succeeded. Inventions often happen because of such a desire.

Who Wants to Fly Anyway?

History tells this tale. In 500 B.C., King Bladud of Britain wanted to fly. The king made some wings out of feathers. He strapped his new wings on. Then he jumped off a cliff. Big mistake! King Bladud crashed to a messy death.

King Bladud used a trial-and-error method for his invention. He tried an experiment. The experiment did not work. Sadly, King Bladud's "error" cost him his life.

---

desire: a strong wish
trial-and-error: the process of trying or testing over and over until the right result is found

The Amazing Leonardo da Vinci

The trial-and-error method works best when inventors research first. That way, they can avoid big errors. They can also gain useful information.

Leonardo da Vinci (1452-1519) invented by using trial-and-error. The Italian was one of the most brilliant people the world has known. He too wanted to invent a way to fly.

Da Vinci observed birds' wings closely. He noted every detail about them. He observed how birds' wings worked. He made drawings of everything he saw. This was all part of his research.

Da Vinci realized that to just make wings wouldn't work. He saw that humans would never be able to fly by flapping wings. So instead, he designed wings with levers and pulleys to help a person fly.

---

brilliant: very smart
lever: a tool that moves something else
pulley: a tool that pulls or lifts

Da Vinci's work even amazes people today. But Da Vinci was too brilliant for his time. No one 500 years ago could make his flying machine. Do you think it could have worked?

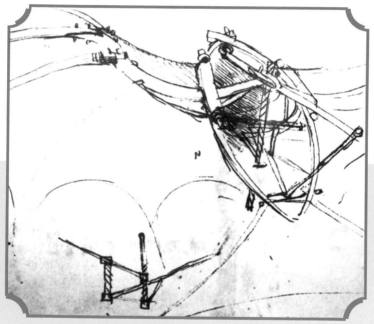

Leonardo da Vinci made drawings of his flying machine.

The "Wright" Way to Fly

By 1903, inventors had newer materials and technology to work with. They also had that same old desire to fly.

The Wright brothers

Brothers Wilbur and Orville Wright ran a bicycle repair business. But they were interested in more than repairing bikes. They started to make gliders. They used the ideas of a German inventor. (He had crashed and died in 1896.) This was part of their research.

The Wright brothers started to build an airplane. They used what they knew about making light, strong gliders. Next, they built a small gasoline engine. The engine produced power to move a bicycle chain. The chain turned two propellers on the edge of the wings.

---

technology: science as it is used in everyday life
glider: a flying machine with no engine
propeller: a set of blades that spin to provide force to make an airplane, ship, or helicopter move

The engine turned the bike chain. The bike chain turned the propellers. And the propellers pushed the plane forward through the air. Orville Wright was flying!

The first flights lasted only a few seconds. Soon, they were lasting much longer. The Wright brothers flew into history.

The first flight of the Wright brothers' plane

Is It a Bird? Is It a Plane?

People had flown before the Wright brothers. In 1709, the King of Portugal got a shock. A priest brought a hot air balloon to the palace. The priest used a flame to fill the balloon with hot air. It rose 13 feet (4 meters) in the air. But the flame nearly set the curtains on fire. So a frightened servant shot the balloon down.

In 1783, a French inventor flew a balloon. The balloon scared the people who saw it. When it landed, they attacked it.

That same year, the French Montgolfier brothers made history by flying a balloon. This flight was the first time living beings flew in a man-made craft. So who were the lucky ones to soar into the sky? They were a sheep, a duck, and a cockerel.

---

cockerel: a young rooster

Flying into the Future?

Today, flying is no big deal. People of da Vinci's time would be totally amazed at planes, rockets, and space stations. What kinds of machines do you think people will use to travel in the future?

The Montgolfier brothers' balloon

Albert Einstein was a scientist.
All scientists are inventors in a way.

CHAPTER 5

Who Invents?

Many inventors are scientists. But inventors can also be people who work in business, music, sports, and many other jobs. Some inventors are even kids! Can you think of any inventions that were made by kids?

From Surfing to Skateboarding

It was the 1960s. Two young surfers from California wanted to practice surfing. But they wanted to be able to surf out of water. So they mixed together roller skates and a surfboard.

They had invented a new sport. First they called it *rollsurf.* By the 1970s, the name had changed to *skateboarding.* Today, kids all over the world are "surfing" on skateboards.

Just like scientists in a laboratory, these two men used what they knew. They set up an experiment. They acted on the results. They became successful inventors!

Louis Braille: Child Inventor

One child inventor has helped millions of people by his work with dots.

Louis Braille was blind from the age of three. He wanted to read. But normal books were no use to him.

The Braille family had a friend who was in the army. In 1823, this army captain showed Louis, age 13, something that changed his life. He showed him how the army sent messages at night.

Soldiers couldn't read messages in the dark. But they could feel them. The army had invented a code soldiers could "read" with their hands in the dark.

The code used dots on paper. Different numbers of dots stood for each letter. The dots were raised above the page. Soldiers could read the dots by feeling them with their fingers.

But the army code did not work well for Louis. It used too many dots. For two years, Louis tried to solve this problem.

Finally, Louis found he could write any symbol with just six dots. His simple, new code worked perfectly. Blind people could now read.

There are 42 million blind people in the world today. Everywhere, people use the Braille system, named after the young boy who invented it.

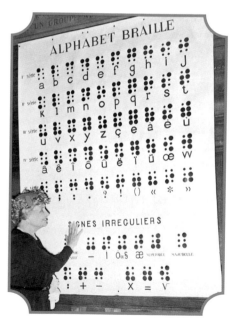

The Braille alphabet

---

symbol: something that stands for something else

Starting Early

As a child, Guglielmo (gool-yee-EL-mo) Marconi was always inventing something. Often he destroyed things, angering his parents! However, Marconi also created things. He invented a machine that made bells ring by catching electricity from storms. He later invented the radio.

In the Dark

Becky Schroeder was waiting in the car while her mom ran errands. She was doing her fifth-grade homework, until it became too dark to see. She wished she had something to help her see her work.

Later, Becky started thinking about things that give off light. She tried mixing together phosphorescent (foss-fuh-RESS-unt) chemicals. She found she could use these chemicals to make a plastic board glow.

---

phosphorescent: giving off light

Becky then added lines to the board. She discovered that the lines glowed through a blank sheet of paper. Her invention, called the Glo-Sheet®, helps people write in straight lines even when there is little or no light.

To be an inventor, you don't need to understand how phosphorescent chemicals work. Simple things can be amazing, too. Remember the wheel! And remember, anyone can be an inventor. How about you?

Becky Schroeder works on an invention.

Becky uses the Glo Sheet she invented.

Epilogue

How to Be an Inventor

So you've got a great idea. What next? First, you need to make careful notes about your idea. It might not work as you planned. Follow the inventing method.

Did your idea work? If so, great! Now you need to find out if anyone else has had the same idea. You could do some research in the library or on the Internet.

If it really is a good, new invention, you can patent it. A patent is a legal right to an invention. It says the invention is yours. You can sell a patent. But no one can take your idea if you patent it first.

In the United States, the U.S. Patent and Trademark Office gives patents. They need to know the idea is new. They also need to know if the idea can be made. If you can prove your idea is both new and possible, they will give you a patent.

When inventors apply for a patent, they often include drawings of how their inventions work.

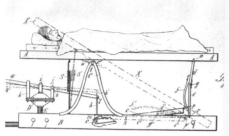

In 1901, Ludwig Ederer invented an alarm bed that tipped to a 45-degree angle when it was time to get up. The person sleeping would get thrown out of bed!

Here is a drawing of a swimming machine that was patented in 1910. The swimmer turned a handle at the front. This turned a propeller under the water.

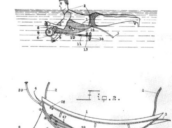

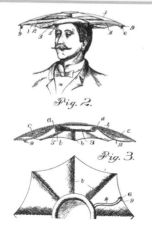

The umbrella hat was invented in 1898 by Joseph Smith. He was able to protect his invention by getting a patent for it.

Glossary

accidentally: by mistake

antibiotic: a drug that cures some infections and diseases

ball: a large, formal dancing party

beggar's-lice: a plant with dry, prickly seed pods that stick to fur and clothing

brilliant: very smart

chemical: a substance produced in chemistry

cockerel: a young rooster

confess: to admit that you did something wrong

criminal: someone who does something against the law

desire: a strong wish

experiment: a scientific test to try out an idea or to see the effect of something

extractor: a machine that takes something out of something else

filament: the fine thread that glows inside a light bulb

glider: a flying machine with no engine

hypodermic syringe: a hollow needle used to give injections under the skin

infection: an illness caused by a germ or virus

laboratory: a special room where scientific work is done

lever: a tool that moves something else

method: a way of doing something

mixture: something made up of different things mixed together

observe: to watch something

patent: to get a legal record that says an invention is your own idea, and that you invented it first

phosphorescent: giving off light

predict: to say what you think might happen

propeller: a set of blades that spin to provide force to make an airplane, ship, or helicopter move

pulley: a tool that pulls or lifts

reaction: an action in response to something

research: to study and find out about something

shock absorber: something that lessens the effect of a jarring force

silicone: a substance found in sand and rocks

symbol: something that stands for something else

technology: science as it is used in everyday life

test tube: a narrow glass tube closed at one end and used to hold liquids

trial-and-error: the process of trying or testing over and over until the right result is found

version: a form of something

Bibliography

Bender, Lionel. *Invention*. Eyewitness Books. New York: DK Publishing, 2000.

Davies, Eryl. *Inventions*. DK Pockets. New York: DK Publishing, 1995.

Erlbach, Arlene. *The Kids' Invention Book*. Minneapolis: Lerner Publications, 1997.

Thimmesh, Catherine. *Girls Think of Everything: Stories of Ingenious Inventions by Women*. Boston: Houghton Mifflin, 2000.

Tucker, Tom. *Brainstorm!: The Stories of Twenty American Kid Inventors*. New York: Farrar, Straus and Giroux, 1995.

VanCleave, Ted. *Totally Absurd Inventions: America's Goofiest Patents*. Kansas City, Mo.: Andrews McMeel Publishing, 2001.

Useful Addresses

The Franklin Institute
222 North 20th Street
Philadelphia, PA 19103

The United States Patent and Trademark Office
General Information Services Division
U.S. Patent and Trademark Office
Crystal Plaza 3, Room 2C02
Washington, DC 20231

Internet Sites

The National Inventors Hall of Fame™
http://www.invent.org/hall_of_fame/1_0_0
_hall_of_fame.asp

Kids' Patent Cafe
http://kids.patentcafe.com/

United States Patent and Trademark Office
http://www.uspto.gov/

Index